VENDING

A True STORY

"If you are thinking about buying a vending machine, then you can't afford not to read this book."

-Greg Joseph

VENDING

A True Story

Copyright © 2021 Greg Joseph

All rights reserved.

No copy of this book may be reproduced, copied, stored in a retrieval system, or transmitted in any form by any means - other than for "fair use" such as reviews or quotations, without the permission from the publisher.

Formatting by Rik – Wild Seas Formatting

Have A Dream, Desire, Or a Plan to Do What You Want With Your Life? Then Do It, Because No One Else Will

Greg Joseph

DEDICATION

To the memory of George Butch Joseph and James Kevin Clougherty.

We're trying guys, but we still can't carry your jock straps.

Greg Joseph and Tom Clougherty, co-owners

Doing what they do best... one more time

PREFACE

This story would not have been possible without the following people. My wife Lynne, who encouraged me to begin this venture in the middle of a recession, while raising our three children. She would later become the office manager for our company. My parents Butch and Jane, who raised myself and four siblings tough enough, while working multiple jobs to maintain the middle-class status we were a part of... not to mention lending me $1700 for our first machine in 1989.

My son Matt, who learned this business at the age of ten and eventually became one of our best employees. My business partner Tom, who was a co-worker of mine at the time I decided to install my first snack vending machine and agreed to join me in this endeavor.

Tom's dad Jim, who was plant manager at the soda distributorship we were working at and was one of our biggest supporters. And, last but not least, the three local vending companies that wouldn't stop whining to our former employer about a conflict of interest, even though we had received permission before installing our first machine. Had the whining stopped, we more than likely would have remained part-timers, something I don't like to think about. Thanks guys.

CONTENTS

THE BEGINNING 1
   STILL LOOKING 2
BULB GOES OFF 5
THE FIRST ACCOUNT 7
LET'S DO THIS 13
MORE 17
AND MORE 23
VACATION = BIG FISH 27
HELP 31
COMPETITION AND SODA 35
FRESH FOOD AND COMMISSIONS 39
FULL-TIME VENDOR 45
   AN ACQUISTION AND REAL ESTATE 46
   FULL-TIME VENDORS 50
GETTING IN 53
CONTRACTS AND CONTACTS 57
A BIG ACQUISITION AND WAREHOUSE 61
FINAL ACQUISITION 67
   SEEN SOME CHANGES 68
THINKING OF SELLING? NAH 73
SELLING? YEAH, AND A FINAL MOVE 77
CONCLUSION 81
GLOSSARY 84
ABOUT THE AUTHOR 91

INTRODUCTION

This book was written as proof that anyone can get into the 30 billion dollar a year vending industry and have success. We did it and so can you. If what you know about vending seems too good to be true, well it is, sort of. Install a machine, fill it and return in a couple of days to collect the booty. That's true, but there's a bunch of other stuff that comes with the territory... and it's one of the reasons I wrote this book.

The other is because I'm selfish. After 38 years in the snack and beverage industry there's a story to tell and I hope you'll enjoy it. Whether you want to operate one or many vending machines, this information will help navigate you through the do's and don'ts when you decide it's your turn. Learn how to acquire quality accounts, the best machines for every location and the best products to sell. Avoid the get rich schemes and the promise of locators finding high traffic areas for their overpriced machines.

You will also learn about commissions, contracts, vehicles, route scheduling, warehousing, repair issues, and the right equipment applications. Then, when you've made enough money and are ready to retire, the final pages of this book will benefit you as well. Please keep in mind that this is the real deal. The names and places weren't changed as to expose the guilty and protect the innocent.

THE BEGINNING

I have had plenty of good jobs in my day but always had the desire to own a business. I worked for state and local government, UPS, Coca-Cola and other places where most people would spend a career. Not being a fan of authority, I wanted to do it my way and my wife was OK with this.

Back in the late eighties the internet wasn't being widely used, so our searches were limited to newspapers, magazines and business brokers for information. Franchises were readily available and we were looking into Dunkin' Donuts. The problem was, we were in New Hampshire and the closest one available was in South Carolina... that wouldn't work. None the less we continued to look for an opportunity.

We needed to make a calculated decision because we were prepared to sell our house to make this happen. We were fortunate that I had a steady job but with three kids and a stay-at-home Mom, we could have used some extra money. I was working at Coca-Cola as a cold drink route driver delivering Coca-Cola products to all types of establishments, with the exception of stores. This meant servicing hospitals, restaurants, gas stations, schools and workplaces.

I delivered cases of soda cans, bottles and tanks of syrup. About 40% of my day was spent filling soda machines. In the beverage industry we call this Full Service. The Coca-Cola company would supply the machines, route drivers would fill the machines, the customers would insert their money (50 cents a can then) and make a purchase. There was a set schedule for refilling these machines and collecting the money (AKA cashing out). Most of these machines were in schools. The authorities weren't monitoring diets back then and the machines could be used anytime of the day. The big sellers were Coke, Diet Coke, Sunkist, Sprite, Pepsi, Mountain Dew and a few pseudo-fruit drinks.

Dentists and the makers of Ritalin loved us. I used to put 50 plus cases in these machines every other day and in hot weather I would have to go daily. I didn't realize it then but that was my start in the vending business. I enjoyed my route and could pump cans into a machine as fast as anyone. This kept me in great shape too, but I still wasn't satisfied.

STILL LOOKING

I came across an ad in the business opportunity column of our local newspaper one day for snack machines. This was a 1-800 number based out of Florida... the boiler room capital of the world. These sales people were trying to sell a counter-top snack machine called the **Snak-Stix**.

First of all, the unit was about the size of a briefcase, you could walk away with it under one arm.

Second, it would not give change and to get an item you had to maneuver a handle with some type of adhesive material (thus the name Snak-Stix) to grab a snack and drop it in the delivery bin.

To this day, one of the craziest things I have ever heard of... can't imagine how many people got ripped off by this scheme. Lucky for me, I couldn't see forking over thousands of dollars to someone in Florida who claimed they could find locations in New Hampshire for me to place these machines, but couldn't tell me exactly where... **1-800 numbers based in Florida are not a good place to start when looking for vending machines**.

Later in this guide, I will list some companies and contact info where you can get quality equipment and service. The vending business has always been a great way to make money, but few people really understand the concept. I kind of knew the game from my job at Coca-Cola and was starting to think this was something I'd like to try, but after some due diligence I decided to move on from SnakStix.

This type of stuff is still going on today, even for full sized vending machines. I advise you to be careful because their ads are convincing. They offer low priced machines and promise a good return on your investment. They will also help place the machines for you in so-called high-volume locations.

Twenty dollars a week is not high volume and is going to take you a while to pay them off. Not only are these machines of low quality, when they break down you will be on your own because there is no service department to assist you. It is not unusual to see an ad for used vending machines, only to find out the seller is someone who unfortunately invested in one of these scams.

BULB GOES OFF

On my Coke route I made deliveries to a couple of vending companies. They would buy soda and lots of it. An owner of one of these companies, A&R Vending, happened to live across the street from me. His name was Rick... just a regular guy who I noticed did pretty well for himself.

Right around this time, I was servicing an account on my route called H&M Metals, when **the guy in charge (contact)** named Squiggy, asked if I knew a vendor that could install a snack machine in their new breakroom. I told him I would tell my neighbor Rick, which I did.

Two weeks later, on my next scheduled service date at H&M Metals when I found out Rick hadn't responded, a bulb went off in my head. I asked Squig if I could get him a snack machine and he said sure. The only problem was, I needed to get one ASAP and I had no idea how that was going to happen, but I told him I could and would call him the next day. This was November of 1989 and was going to be the start of a 30-plus year career in the vending business.

THE FIRST ACCOUNT

Now that I had stumbled upon my first vending account, time was of the essence. I needed to get a snack machine so I used a very common resource at the time, the Yellow Pages (remember phone books?).

I found a distributor not too far away and gave them a call. After I explained my situation, the salesman asked if I would be interested in selling the account instead. I had already thought it would be a good account based off the soda sales they were doing, so I said no.

The bulb in my head just got brighter. I got all the information and told him I needed an hour or two to figure some things out. The main thing on my mind, was how to pay for this snack vending machine and also the product to fill it. Not to mention, getting permission to do this from the plant manager.

Unenviable tasks at the time. I knew something about filling soda machines, but nothing about snack machines with the exception of buying a bag of chips... just like other human beings on the planet.

The salesman assured me the person delivering the machine would walk me through the install and to make sure we had quarters, dimes and nickels for the **coin mech** (this would allow change to be dispensed).

MEI coin mechs – 3 tube and 5 tube – top notch in the industry

Forgetting to bring coin for installs was something we did probably five or six times in over thirty years in business. Not too bad. One thing about this business is just when you think you've seen or done everything, especially with service calls, you're going to find you haven't. After a brief discussion with my wife I decided to ask one of my co-workers if he was interested in going in on this with me.

We were friends and in a similar situation with our families and finances. We would each have to invest $1700 to buy the snack machine **(a U-Select-It or U.S.I.)** and the product to go in it.

I now had a business partner and his name was Tom. Now the hard part, getting the O.K. from our boss, Tom's dad.

We stated it was a snack vendor with no soda involved and were told there wouldn't be a problem. I borrowed the money from my parents and Tom emptied his bank account. We figured we would give this business a try and if it didn't work out, we could sell the account and at least break even. We scheduled the installation for a Monday at 4:00 pm. Our first route truck was a **1971 Volkswagon camper bus**.

1971 VW Camper Bus, Joseph family vehicle and the company's first route truck. Note: Red house in background belonged to Rick (A&R Vending) – thanks Rick

This was also my family buggy at the time. On that Monday we finished our regular jobs and picked up the stock we would need from a local wholesaler. We bought cases of all brand name items... stuff like Lay's, Hershey, Mars, Hostess cakes, etc. The salesman at the vending machine company did a thorough job **planning the install** with us. First floor or second floor? Ground level or dock height? And, every vendors enemy, stairs?

Yes, there were 16 of them, but a straight shot without doors (another enemy). In this business you should always have a tape measure, especially when you are checking out a potential account. Be ready to take off doors, take out windows, go up and down stairs, take doors off machines, slide machines on moving blankets and doing whatever it takes to get a 500+ pound machine where you need it to be.

One particular install we did early on was with a small pick up truck Tom owned. It was for a school where we had to unload the machine and enter the cafeteria at ground level because the loading dock was out of service. After about five seconds of scratching our heads, we noticed a set of double doors on the building off of the courtyard. Tom, being the expert driver he is, drove the truck through the doors and across the floor of the cafeteria and we were able to complete the install. Better than waiting for another day, isn't it?

Sometimes a facility manager will lend a hand but you should be aware of all of the above before you even order a machine. It's awfully tough to fit a 34" wide machine through a 32" wide door opening. The delivery driver from the vending machine company showed up by himself. Big guy and experienced. It took him about an hour and a half to get the machine off his truck and into place using an **electric stair climber**.

He gave Tom and I a few bits of advice and he was on his way. Three hours later after loading the machine and performing several test vends we were on our way. After an install and every service call be sure to **perform several test vends** to ensure the machine(s) are working properly. The talk on the way home was that if this machine made us a few bucks we would see if we could place a few more to supplement our current incomes. We returned to my house to put away the leftover stock in **my garage (our first warehouse)** and had a couple beers.

LET'S DO THIS

The next day at work seemed different than the norm. We couldn't tell anyone at the facility what we were up to because quite frankly, we didn't know if it was going to work out. Thursday was our first scheduled service visit and it couldn't have come fast enough. This account had two shifts and about 135 employees. We picked up the stock in my garage just in case the machine needed refilling. When we got to the machine it was more than half empty. Machines that accepted dollar bills were new to the vending industry at that time and when we emptied the 3" thick wad of bills from the **bill stacker** and dumped out a bucket of coins, we looked at each other and said, "let's do this." The new snack machine was a hit not only with us but the employees as well. This visit took us half the time to refill the machine and that was three days after the initial install. Our next visit was scheduled for Monday. The account would have to be done twice a week, Monday and Thursday.

  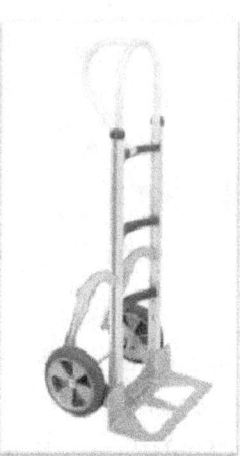

Tools of the trade. Electric stair climber, 4 wide USelect It (U.S.I.) 1st machine we bought and a Magliner hand truck (the best out there)

The service frequencies we used were: daily (which would most always include a fresh food machine), Monday and Thursday or Tuesday and Friday (accounts like H&M Metals), one day a week or every other week (for smaller locations doing $50 - $75 a week). A good rule of thumb is to **try to schedule servicing machines so you are taking out at least $75 - $100 every visit.**

We headed back to my house to count the money (by hand). That one snack machine did about $175 in less than three days. The weekly takes were $250 - $275. We didn't have to be veterans in the industry to know this was a good one and quickly understood why someone would want to buy it. Now, lots of times in this industry you won't take the account if you can't get the soda business as well but we were just starting out and were restricted from selling soda because of our jobs. Soda is where the money is.

My contact at H&M serviced the soda machine and had a nice slush fund going for himself but we didn't care. We had ourselves a very good snack account and were hungry for more. Years later when Squiggy retired, he let us take over the soda machines and it became an even better account. We are still in this account thirty-three years later... longevity unheard of in this industry. Lots of workplaces change vending companies every 3 -5 years, we must have been doing something right.

MORE

It wasn't long before we had settled in at H&M Metals. We were comfortable operating the machine and received feedback on what snacks our customers liked and wanted. As I said, my soda route consisted of any establishment except stores... all potential vending accounts. I had a very good relationship with everyone on my route and it wasn't hard to sell them on my new part-time business as a snack vendor. The next account I landed was down the street from H&M, an Emergency Med-Stop. Due to space constraints, we put in a compact **snack machine (USI)** about 4' tall and 20" wide, much smaller than our first machine. If it emptied, we'd probably pull $50 out of it.

Facsimile of a U.S.I compact vendor.

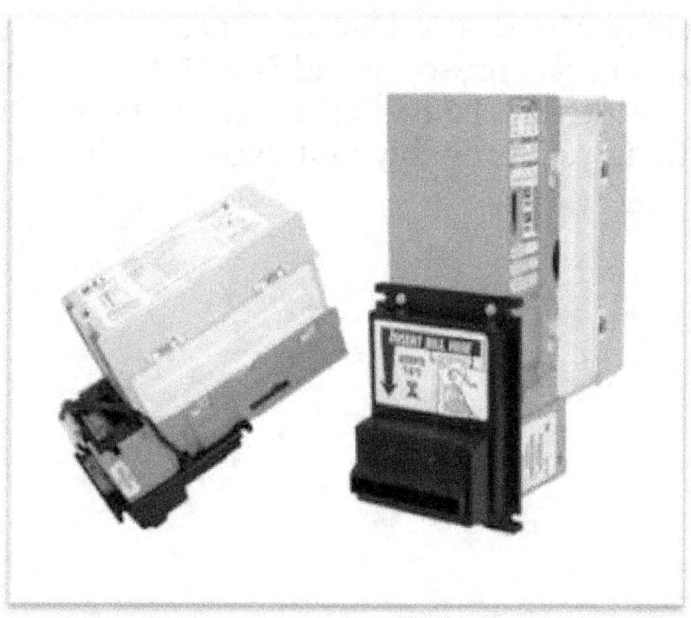

MEI 1&5 dollar bill acceptor. Like the coin mechs, top notch.

5 Wide Automatic Products (AP) snack and one of the best ever made.

We didn't care though because it was another account. It didn't take us long to avoid these small machines unless it was part of a big account with several locations within one large facility. We call these **satellites** in the industry. The account does very good volume, so if they want another machine at the other end of the building where there are a few employees distanced from the main cafeteria, you get them a smaller machine(s). It's all part of doing business because if you don't, a competitor will. We still have this account as well (30+ yrs) and also do the soda. We have upgraded to a full-size snack with all the bells and whistles.

You should always know the wants and needs of your locations because they can change.

Accounts that grow may need more and or larger equipment and a reduced workforce may result in downgrading or removing some equipment. This is not only important for your bottom line but the account as well.

Remember, if you get into the vending business, you're also in the moving business. Because this was a compact machine, we were able to pick it up at the dealer with the VW bus and after some instruction, we installed it ourselves, quick learners. Once our second account was up and running, I already knew where I wanted to place a third machine… in an industrial park down the street from our first account. The owners gave us the OK and agreed to a used machine. I pushed for a used machine because we couldn't really afford new at every location and this was a bunch of rough necks that didn't mind kicking the machine now and again.

Always keep a multi-purpose spray bottle in your truck or machine(s) to clean any blemishes while servicing an account. It does happen. This location was an older factory with two shifts and 50+ people. The only thing the owners cared about was to make sure we put in peanut M&M's. Understood. I knew exactly where I was going to get the machine.

At the Coke plant where we worked, we would gas up at a Texaco station right down the road and they had an empty snack machine in the back of the building. We were able to buy it for $300, a great deal even then. This was a **5 wide (amount of snack columns) Automatic Products (AP)** snack vendor and it was in great shape. No **bill validator** but as I said, there were lots of machines in the field that still didn't have them and the company's owner didn't really care.

Later on while soliciting accounts, we were successful in landing quite a few of them because 75% of the machines we purchased were new and were equipped with **bill acceptors (validators).** We had a slight problem with this next install in that this machine was too big for the VW bus.

Our bosses at Coke would let employees use the pick-up trucks for personal use like moving appliances or furniture. A vending machine can be classified as furniture, right? And that's what we thought. So, one Wednesday night with the help of the gas station's owners we had that machine on the truck in about 20 minutes and were on our way to set up our third account. We were building a nice little business for ourselves.

AND MORE

Our fourth account was another factory called All-Tex. This place did metal casting and walking through the plant the temperature would hover around 100 degrees plus, a challenging work environment. One interesting thing about the vending business is getting to see and learn about different workplaces. Over the years, I made many contacts in different industries and was able to help friends and relatives get job opportunities, though not at All-Tex. This location had around 30 employees, so we needed another small machine. We didn't want to buy new because we now had a good grasp on projecting sales volume and usage. Thirty blue collar guys back then would spend about a dollar a day in vending machines, so we were looking at maybe $25-$30 a week because sans soda. We were missing out on the soda revenue early on but it didn't matter to us.

We were in this part-time and a lot of our early snack accounts came as a result of our jobs with arguably the biggest vending company in the world, Coca-Cola. Giving up vending soda for getting a good base of snack accounts seemed like a fair trade to us, and it was. We had no idea but down the road we'd end up servicing most of those soda machines as well. Working for Coca-Cola taught us valuable lessons we would use in the vending industry. Give the best service to the customer, who is always right, keep a neat appearance and get the job done. And very important, if a customer or account claims they're owed money lost in a machine, pay it without any argument.

Most failed vends are the result of user error but do you want to chance losing an account over 1 or 2 dollars? Few people want free money from the vendor but there are some. You'll figure this out soon enough and after a quick discussion with your **contact (you should have one in every account),** any issues can be worked out. The only questions we ask are: which machine, item and how much do we owe you? If possible, we would replicate the same vend choice with the customer.

Lots of times, there's no problem. And if there is, fix it, run a few test vends and be on your way. Believe it or not, we were able to land new accounts because the current vendor complained about reimbursement money. At the end of the day in this business, trust me, you're way ahead. The machine we put in at All-Tex was a **Crane National and built the same as a cigarette vendor**. You would insert money and pull one of the 8-10 knobs for an item to drop, pretty much now an antique. This machine has been called the best vendor ever built, couldn't destroy it with dynamite and for it's small size weighed about 400 pounds. The only issue was exact change only, which was OK because most of our products were vending for .50 and change was plentiful. We paid $150 for the machine and the weekly take was a surprise at around $65.

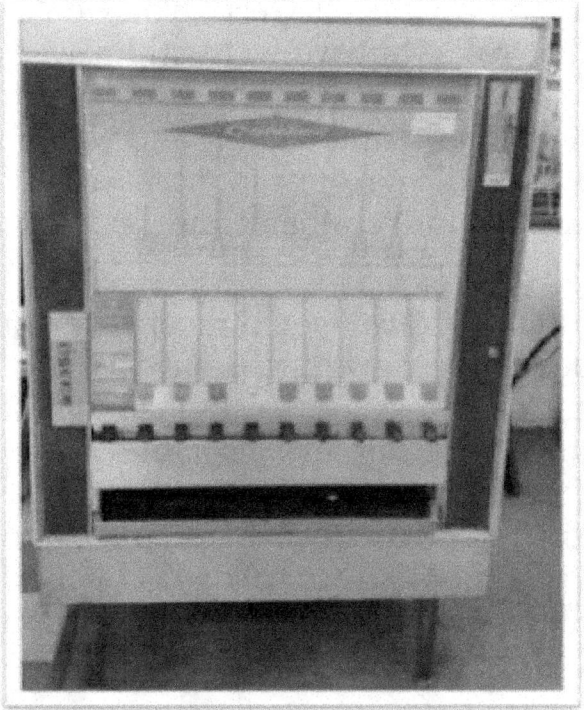

Crane National pull knob and arguably the best ever made.

We were really getting to like this. By now we were doing a new install at least once a month. Equipment dealers and product wholesalers started reaching out to us and we didn't even have a name for the company. We had a friend in the business (and there weren't many),Gerry, who'd been around for many years and would share his knowledge with us about the industry. He would sell us used equipment as well.

Over the years we bought lots of nice machines at a fair price and we wouldn't take an account from him unless he didn't want it. During this time we were taking most any size account to increase cash flow and any new locations Gerry didn't want he would give us their information. We had a nice relationship. Once you've been doing this as long as Gerry, you won't take every account that calls, but we were still a ways off from that. At the time, it was unthinkable but years later we'd end up buying his company and warehouse when he retired. Over the next few months we landed a VFW hall, a granite foundry, a bank and a nursing home, all snack machines.

Monday after work, we would meet at my house, load the product in the now gutted out VW bus and bang out the snack route we were establishing. Fortunately, the accounts were all in the same area, about 25 minutes from my house. This would take around 3 hours and then we'd head back and count out the money (no **coin counter** yet) on my kitchen table. My wife would deposit it in our checking account the next day.

VACATION = BIG FISH

By now our co-workers were starting to figure things out and we wanted to make sure we were still OK with the plant manager, Tom's dad Jim. We reiterated what we had going on and were told that as long as we did our jobs, there wouldn't be a problem. We were working an extra 3-4 hours a week in our new business and had been at it for 4 months. Still, no name for the company and no business plan either. We never really developed a long term business plan, for us it was what do we have to do today and what's on tap for tomorrow. Looking back, pretty good strategy. We were thinking of keeping this part-time or maybe hiring someone to run the route. We were a ways off from supporting two families and weren't even taking out any money yet. I had a week vacation at the time and decided to go out and **cold call new business (when you knock on the door of an establishment and make a sales pitch**), figuring maybe we could build this up some more and start paying ourselves a little bit of money. By now we knew what locations were the good ones. As far as general workplaces, whichever parking lots had the most cars. No rocket science here. But the best ones were schools grades 7-12, the more students the better. Coca-Cola and Pepsi had a lock on the drinks but snacks were up for grabs. That week I cold called two of the biggest schools in the state and landed both of them. A real good get. By now, we had financing with equipment distributors and product wholesalers. We put 5 wide **U-Selects** in each school and there was always a constant stream of business. At this point in time, our two best accounts. Keep in mind that back then the uber intellects weren't blaming the refreshment industry for students being overweight. We knew it wouldn't last forever because kids were buying a candy bar, bag of chips and a soda for lunch, but we did have a nice run. Nowadays the rules have changed but schools are still good accounts. The suppliers have done a good job producing healthier, low fat, low sugar and low cal items. Some schools will want the machines off during class hours but will keep them on before and after school with no restrictions. Some leave them on all day as long as the products being sold are on the **school healthy federal government list,** while others will want the machines off during lunch periods. Different rules for different schools so be aware. **Any machine in a school is going to need a timer,** but even with these limitations you'll be surprised at how well they will do.

5-wide U-Select

I really believe people, especially young people, like using vending machines because they see all the items behind the glass and are in total control. No clerk to deal with, kinda like a power thing. That's until they don't get an item because it hangs up and then beat the crap out of your machine. Not everything is gravy. You can eliminate most hang ups by loading the product the right way. If you have to force an item into a spiral it probably won't vend. That's why **testing your machines before you leave the location after install is important.** Machines today can test vend every column rather quickly in **service mode.** Remember this motto: **keep em cleaned, filled and working.**

HELP

Once revenue started coming in from the schools, we were able to hire a part-time employee and we needed one. We also bought much needed **coin and bill counters**. My wife was becoming more involved in office work and my retired father Butch assumed the money counting duties. The money was counted and recorded per account then brought to the bank.

Cash and coin counters. When you need these, you're on your way.

This is a copy of one of our money counting pages.

The business was starting to spread out logistically so Tom and I stayed on the Monday run and our employee, his cousin Linda, would service the two schools out of her car. Other changes were buying a 1986 Chevy Van, more warehouse space (a vacant first floor apt. in a building Tom owned) and a name for the company --- **Premium Vending Inc.**

That bottom apartment was once our warehouse. Thanks T.C.

We landed a few more accounts that Linda serviced and decided to keep running this as a side business. We were about 8 months into our venture. I must admit that the possibility of becoming a full-time vendor was still a thought, but things were going well and we were able to start taking $200 dollars each week for our efforts. Our stay in

Big step up from a 1971 V.W.

Tom's building was short lived however, as he was able to rent out the apartment. We would move two more times before buying our first warehouse. Moving your place of business isn't half bad in this industry because you just wind down the inventory and start getting deliveries at the new location. Obviously, the more accounts the more product the more equipment the more space. Why pay for space you don't need?

COMPETITION AND SODA

Everything was moving along fine until one day we were called into Jim's office. Word was out on the streets that a couple of Coke guys were servicing their own vending machines. The owner of one of the larger local vending companies called the plant voicing concerns about a conflict of interest. We assured the boss that we were still only doing snack vendors and the call was pretty much ignored.

I actually got the feeling that Jim was proud of us for not only being good employees, but also trying to do better for ourselves. At that time, we decided not to grow the business anymore and would put someone on full time. We would manage what we had and continue working at Coca-Cola. This plan didn't last long because soon, other vendors started calling in trying to protect their turf as well. Throughout our career we never called anyone relating to competition or losing an account. If we lost an account, and there weren't many, we'd look in the mirror first, then ask each other why.

Unless someone undercuts pricing or bumps up a **commission (money given back to the account based on sales)** losing an account is on you, the vendor. You have to ask yourself why, correct the problem and learn from the mistake. We believed that competition made us better. You will have competition too but if you do the job and concentrate on your business, you'll be fine. There are times you can lose an account because your contact leaves and the replacement has a relationship with another service. This happens, though not frequently. Nothing you can do except work out a smooth transition and leave on good terms.

We had this happen a few times over thirty years and were called back twice because the new company didn't match our service. Don't burn the bridge. We never did, although we did blow one up. We received a call from a circuit board company that was interested in a snack machine for their newly remodeled break room. I met with the owner and was asked if the machine could mirror the break rooms décor, mainly the cabinets which had wood grain fronts. At that time, most all of the new vendors came stock with that particular look, so this was really a no brainer.

I ordered the machine from our distributor and it was at the location three days later, brand new and in the shipping area. Myself and Tom's uncle Roger, a retired policeman that would help us out now and again, went over to do the install. After uncrating the vendor, we began moving it into the break room via **pallet jack** when the owner stopped by to check out the machine. Just as I proudly began to show it off, he started screaming that it wasn't the right look. Now I'm no interior decorator, but the match looked pretty damn good to me.

After minutes of trying to reason with the guy and save the account, he finally tells us he doesn't want the machine. At this point I'm thinking, I really couldn't provide service to a jerk like that so I tell him what's really on my mind… and it wasn't all that good. We begin wheeling the machine out with the pallet jack and he's following us, still spewing nonsense. Being quite proficient handling moving equipment I found an opportunity to run over one of his feet and did so, to the tune of about 750 pounds of hard steel. In an obvious state of pain, he starts yelling for someone to call the police and I'm trying to offer up a totally fake apology. Roger settles the guy down by telling him he's an ex-policeman and he'll take care of everything, whatever that meant and the owner limps off. As we're putting the machine back on the truck, employees that witnessed the incident start discretely congratulating us and giving us a thumbs up.

At that point I honestly felt pretty good because it was obvious this jack-ass got what he deserved, even if we didn't get the account. It hurt a little bit but not for long, me that is. When we started this business, we were the new kids on the block and the four local vending companies didn't want any more competition. They were stuck in the past and this industry is always moving forward. Actually, it was pretty easy getting new business. If you follow trends, stay up on new equipment and stay in touch with your contacts, you will be able to maintain your accounts for a long time. After the last round of calls to our workplace by the established local vendors,

I knew my days as a Coke employee were numbered. Tom wasn't so sure because he had just been promoted to cold drink manager and ironically one of his tasks was working with vending companies. Crazy, but true.

At this point because of my situation, we made a decision to go after the cold drink segment of the business. Getting the cases was tough because we had to pick them up at gas stations, Wal-Mart and other retailers that had decent pricing. This wasn't too bad because the end game was a noticeable increase in cash flow.

Another hardship was having to purchase our own drink machines because technically, we still weren't selling soda. We made it work by financing new and getting good deals on used, mainly from Gerry. In our area both Coke and Pepsi will loan machines as long as you have an account set up and buy the product from them. Not the lowest pricing but it gets delivered and at our peak we were servicing 300 plus soda machines. At a cost of $2500-$3000 new, you can see it's a great deal.

They also helped with repairs, had rebate programs, would run deals on case lots and gave us event tickets throughout the year. If the same policies hold true in your area, I suggest you take full advantage of this. Coca-Cola gave us our start, so much loyalty there but Pepsi is a great outfit as well. We developed nice relationships with both companies that continue to this day. They've also given us many leads on new business (snack and soda) throughout the years.

FRESH FOOD AND COMMISSIONS

As I mentioned before, **the best places to solicit will have lots of cars in the parking lot**. Plain and simple, so this is what I focused on while cold calling. There was an old mill building in town that I had never thought about until trying to grow this business. The current vendor in there had old equipment and I knew modern machines would get us the account. Lynne wrote up a **proposal** and we were in. This company, Felton Brush had 150 people and 3 shifts. **Second and third shifts do very well in the industry if you can find them anymore.** This was another good one. At this time we were doing an install or two a month and we now had two part-time employees, with Tom and I still servicing our core accounts. We also bought a **1979 Ford rack body with a power tailgate for equipment moves.** It cost $3500, was in great shape and a workhorse.

Getting ready for an install. Definitely need one of these if you're gonna move machines in house.

As I said, **in the vending business you're in the moving business.** And if you hire out moves, it's $200 plus per machine. More machines and stairs means more money. We probably used a mover five times and that was because there were too many stairs. **Electric stair climb dollies** are expensive and not very easy to operate so find a dependable mover and sub out these types of moves. Why risk a severe injury? Many businesses have fork trucks and freight elevators available to lessen the load and equipment dealers will drop ship machines to a desired location as part of the sale. I'm going to estimate we moved about a million pounds of steel (machines) in our career and fortunately no major injuries but many a sore body part, while saving a ton of money.

This account, Felton Brush, came with a couple of firsts for us, a **cold food vendor** and 2 **fresh brew coffee machines.** As well as a snack, 2 cold drinks, a bill changer and 2 microwaves with stands in the main cafeteria. This is called **a full line** in the vending business. A satellite location had another cold drink and coffee machine. Our biggest account as far as equipment thus far. We bought a used drink machine from Gerry and financed the new equipment over 3 years with **Betson Of New England (Canton,Mass.),** another good company for doing business. The net income from the account made the equipment payment, paid the commission (10% gross sales less food vendor) and still provided plenty of cash flow. Regarding commissions, most of our accounts didn't ask for one and we certainly wouldn't bring the topic up.

Why give away hard earned money? Some accounts will ask for a commission to cover the cost of utilities for the machines or to help set up a slush fund for holiday parties, etc. The amount is negotiable, but usually 5-15% of gross sales. Schools will use the money for whatever needs they have that your taxes might not pay for.

Most schools and any government contracts will require a commission (anywhere from 5-40%), but you can still earn a great living if you want to avoid these types of accounts. The majority of locations want good service and fair pricing. Our philosophy through the years was unless we bought used equipment, we would finance all new usually over 3 years. The keys here are a low monthly payment, positive cash flow and keeping the account. Losing an account means extra work picking up machines at the end of the day or weekends and storing them in your warehouse, not making any money. Like many industries, vending is no different when it comes to favorable financing, so be on the lookout for this.

Full Line AKA Bank of Equipment

Upon landing this account we were faced with a major challenge in finding fresh food for the coldfood machine. Our main supplier, **VSA (Vistar of New England)** sold some frozen items we could use like hot pockets, bagels, muffins, breakfast sandwiches, etc. but for this account we needed fresh sandwiches as well. Some of the bigger vending companies were making their own food back then but margins were slim and you needed several accounts to make it work.

Later, most vendors figured out that buying fresh food from commissaries and caterers was more feasible than making it themselves. These days, VSA sells vacuum packed sandwiches that are very good but don't be afraid to shop around for other sources of fresh food in your area.

A local commissary or caterer is always worth a try as long as the food is packaged properly and has an expiration date, usually a six day shelf life. Variety and pricing are very important. Keep pricing affordable and accept feedback from your customers as to what they like. Your food machine mark ups aren't as high as snack, soda and coffee but if you price and merchandise right, you can make a nice profit with this type of machine.

With one food vendor, we had only one option and that was to have my wife Lynne make the food. Tom's wife Karla would wrap fresh donuts just like the current vendor. The town we lived in had only one restriction and that was no trucks making deliveries to our house. No problem, we would pick up the goods. Our contact stated that the employees were buying about 25-30 sandwiches and 2-3 dozen donuts a week which we figured wouldn't be a problem keeping up with.

The first day of operation we got a call saying the food machine was almost empty after the first shift. We all worked into the late afternoon and evening making sandwiches for the second and third shifts, as well as inventory for the following day. The employees loved the food and we were selling five times what we were told. Not a bad thing. With the sale of every sandwich customers would buy a drink, bag of chips and often times a candy bar.

We were doing very well in our first full line account. Snacks and sodas are the way to go in this business but if you do take on food accounts, make sure you're paying lots of attention to the food machines because if you don't, you can be out the door real quick. In full line accounts the food vendor is the heart of the operation and can make or break you.

The norm in the industry is to not pay commissions on food machines due to any spoilage at the end of shelf life, but be sure your contact is aware of this. At our peak we had 16 food vendors in the field and all of these locations understood this agreement. This new account required everyday service because of the food machine, which I would do at 6a.m. on my way into Coca-Cola. We were able to service the rest of the machines every other day. At this point we were working our asses off, around 12-15 extra hours in addition to our regular jobs. We were at a point where one of us could earn a living and pay for benefits if need be. My wife was badgering me to either do this full-time or sell what we had attained because of the work load.

FULL-TIME VENDOR

The Coca-Cola distributorship we worked at was part of a large corporation based in Japan. Today, I believe it is one of the largest bottlers / distributors in the USA. The local vending companies wouldn't stop crying and decided to voice their complaints to corporate which led to a meeting between Tom, Jim, myself and one of their fat cat administrators. After a heated discussion, cooler heads prevailed and it was decided I would leave Coca-Cola and run P.V.I. on a full time basis. We were given a time frame of 6 months to make this happen and were promised the vending service at the plant (no Pepsi of course). You can't make this up.

Being an employee at Coke and doing business with both companies was instrumental in our long careers as vendors. These two beverage giants can only help you. Four months after that meeting I left Coke and was running P.V.I. with mixed emotions. I was anxious because I had never written a paycheck for myself and we really hadn't been in the vending business that long, though 6 years working for Coke was a great start.

For me it was kind of surreal because I was now an owner of a business, albeit with a partner, something I always wanted to do. Throw a bit of pride in there too because of what we had accomplished in only 14 months--- and we worked for it. In the end we outlasted all those companies as well. Three folded and we bought out the other two, A&R and our friend Gerry. It was a twist of fate Rick, of A&R, didn't follow up on the lead I gave him because that would be our first of many accounts in the vending industry. In 30 plus years we NEVER neglected to follow up a call for business.

AN ACQUISTION AND REAL ESTATE

It didn't take long in the vending / beverage industry to hear about this new company whose owners worked for Coca-Cola. Tom stayed on board at Coke because legally corporate was only concerned about one of us leaving and that would be me, I started the business. I was able to draw a weekly pay from P.V.I. and our workloads were comparable with Tom still working for P.V.I. behind the scenes.

We did have to hire a full-time employee and buy another route truck but it was all good, we were heading in the right direction. I was still servicing our original route, doing service calls and going after new business. It wasn't long before we were making more money than we had working for Coca-Cola. We would supplement Tom's pay with monies from P.V.I., while still maintaining a nice checking account.

We had two full-time routes with Tom and our part-timer doing schools and a few other accounts close by. We were running efficiently and still growing, usually one or two new accounts a month. I received a call one day from a vendor in another part of the state that wanted out but only had a small number of accounts left in our territory.

He did have fifty or so machines in storage that needed to be removed, so for short money, we bought him out. It was a good deal because we were able to salvage the few decent accounts left in the field, but more important was getting the machines in storage. A lot of these machines only needed a good cleaning and some refurbishing before we would put them out on location. The rest were used for parts, all for pennies on the dollar. In the industry today, you can take an older machine and put on a new door that is called a **revision door.**

This, and painting the cabinet will give you a brand new looking machine. Revision doors have L.E.D. lights, updated motors, control boards and payment systems. If you're not in the business, you'd think the machine was right from the factory and all for less than 30% cost of a new machine.

We would get our doors from Vendors Exchange in Cleveland, Ohio ,a company we've done business with for over thirty years. They sell everything you'll need in this business, especially parts, whether you have one machine or a thousand.

Revision doors. Totally genius.

They also sell new and used equipment and have a sales team that branches out across the country. Another great company to deal with.

This purchase was well timed because we had just landed two more **full-line** accounts and needed more equipment. Warehouse space was becoming an issue as well due to steady growth. One day I saw a building for sale in a part of town we were familiar with. It was a 45x85 two story barn and was an eye sore in the neighborhood.

The first warehouse that we owned, and like I said, an eye-sore.

Eye-sore no more.

We went through it with a contractor and were told it had a solid frame and roof but needed siding, doors and updated electrical work. We secured some financing from the owner and bought our first warehouse. If you can own, it's always better than paying rent because if the business fails (and it won't if you follow these guidelines) you'll have some real estate to fall back on. Plus, a great feeling of accomplishment because we did a lot of the work there ourselves and increased the property value quickly.

If you can't sell your route(s) when times up in the vending business, you're left with a bunch of scrap metal. Machines that cost $3000 new will be worth $1000, if you're lucky. We ran lean, worked frequently 6-7 days a week and when our checking account was up to it, we'd buy a piece of real estate. We were lucky and only got burned once in 30 years. Pay yourself first when you have cash flow, because it's your business and you should be doing the bulk of the work.

There will come a time when you've had enough, or someone will make an offer you can't refuse and you will sell. We didn't have a pension plan but were lucky enough to pull off a few good deals in the real estate market. Looking back, it was a business plan we never thought of early on but just implemented along the way. When our warehouse was ready, we leased to own a walk in freezer and refrigerator due to an increased volume in food sales. By then we had found a local commissary that had sandwiches comparable to my wife's, which were very good. As I mentioned, food accounts do high volume but require high maintenance.

FULL-TIME VENDORS

One morning our part-time employee informed us he was calling it quits and I totally understood. His route was becoming too heavy due to increased growth. At this time, Tom decided to give his notice at Coca-Cola and join me in running P.V.I. on a full-time basis. It was 1992 and about ten months after my departure. Beside running a route, Tom would deal with people issues like employees, sales contacts, and I would deal with non people issues like equipment, service, trucks. It was a good fit.

Going to work those days was a lot of fun even though we'd still have to deal with customers losing money, equipment moves on a day's notice, replacing shattered glass on a machine from a head butt, winters in New England, etc. etc. Just a few negatives but overall, a rewarding business. At this time we were running 3 routes using ½ **ton Toyota cab over trucks**.

We ended up with over 300k miles on them and our converted barn was still efficient for us. As far as route vehicles go, our philosophy was if we were spending too much money on repairs it was time to trade or sell. We would look for zero percent interest on new, or nice used vehicles with low miles. We would shelve them out ourselves and install heavily insulated coolers that would keep temperature for 8 hours for cold food packages.

Equipment moves were done with our **79 Ford rack body,** which was paid for. All 3 routes were heavy and we probably could've used another part-timer but there was always that paranoia of failing, and this kept us hustling as we moved forward. We were making real good money and it was all cash because card readers weren't available. We did have some accounts receivable for **office coffee service (OCS)** under our terms, which meant high net profit. We found that the OCS business was everchanging with low margins, so we basically cherry picked that part of the business we wanted.

GETTING IN

You can get into the vending business alone or with a partner(s) like I did. One nice account can make you some good money and more accounts can make real good money. You can also purchase an established company which will set you back a certain amount of dollars. Vending companies sell anywhere between .25 and 1.00 per gross dollar depending on variables such as cash flow, equipment, types of accounts, contracts, commissions, trucks and anything else that might be negotiable. Let's say an operator is doing 200k in gross sales a year and everything is new with quality locations, it's quite possible the asking price could be $200k.

This wouldn't include warehouse product, product in the machines, money in the coin mechs and one final cash out by the seller. The same gross sales with older equipment, smaller locations, beat up trucks and you're probably looking at $75-95k or less, around .40 on the gross dollar. One thing I would avoid is dealing with a 1-800#, or anyone from a distance that promises you'll get rich after they help with finding you locations. You know your territory better than anyone hours away. You can do very well in this industry but can also get burned. Everyone's situation is different. How much money to invest? How much money do you want to make? And how much time can you put into the business?

The beauty of vending is you start making money as soon as you fill that first machine and close the door. As long as you make the right choice(s) of where to place your machine(s) and service them properly, you'll be fine. And if you make the wrong choice (and you will if you're in it long enough), you can always find another location for it.

This holds true if you happen to lose an account as well. Buy a **C-Store**, restaurant, health club, gas station, etc. and for whatever reason sales go in the tank, you're screwed. In vending, you have movable sales clerks (machines) that show up every day, give no back talk and work 24/7 365 days of the year, even while you sleep. Not all peaches and cream but if you work it, a pretty damn good business whether it be part-time or full-time. Do not forget though, it's entirely based on service so if you're not able to provide this, you should try another gig.

I would recommend getting a partner because it's easier as you start getting more accounts, especially moving machines around. You'll be on your time, not the movers and won't have to fork over $250 plus for every move. I really believe our accounts liked the fact that not only did we solicit them, we'd install and service them as well. Kept everything tightly knit. If you do buy an established company, make sure you hold back some monies for an agreed time period (usually a year), because a lot to do with keeping accounts is based not only on service but good faith as well. If an account you purchase gets another vendor for any reason other than your poor service, a percentage of the gross sales for the rest of the year should be deducted from the money being held, or your final payment.

Make sure you are introduced to **whoever is in charge (contact)** in all locations and give them a means to contact you with any issues that might arise. Our top locations had our cell numbers, and any problems were addressed quickly.

We had small labels on the front of our machines that included company name, phone number, E mail address and a 24hr. service notice. There are vendors that don't put this information on their machines, I've seen it, and don't get it. Even if the account has a means to reach you, many times a customer will have an issue and with no one to call, they'll do what they think is the next best thing. Kick and or shake your machine. All our accounts knew we were always available. If you don't respond to a service call this is not good. We landed many locations because the vendor would be late or not even respond at all.

Now, with current technology the new machines and revision doors will alert the office computer or your I phone of most problems in a location. Genius, but you still have to communicate and take care of the problem. And believe it or not, some vendors still won't do this. If an account knows you are aware of a problem, this can buy time and you may need it to get the machine in working order. Ordering parts, waiting for a service tech, or worst scenario swapping out a machine, could be one of the remedies.

Troubleshooting vending equipment today is much easier than earlier years because of the I phone and Google.

The equipment manufacturers have service techs you can call and they'll do a nice job of working you through most issues. High ticket items like compressors, control boards, motors and other major components have good warrantees so lots of times it's basically an exchange. Coke and Pepsi will help with most service issues as long as you're buying product from them and are a valued customer. Don't let the fear of fixing a broken machine put a damper on any desire to get into this business. Most of the time you'll swap out a part and be on your way. Make a note or store it in your memory bank because you might run into the same problem again. When ordering parts, order a spare if feasible so you can eliminate next day delivery costs down the road. If you can turn a screwdriver, use a wrench, and have a desire to succeed, you'll be able to handle most repair issues.

CONTRACTS AND CONTACTS

With three heavy routes, we were putting out as much product as any independent vending company in northern New England. We added an office and money counting room in our warehouse and had become a major player in our territory. We started to receive **bids for government locations such as colleges, prisons, airports and highway rest stops.**

These opportunities usually were high volume, involved lots of equipment and were awarded to the company that would pay back the highest commission. Some of these would amount to 30-40%, a lot of money. You could inflate vend prices higher than the norm to help cover the commission but we felt with all the red tape involved, it wouldn't be a good fit for us at the time.

We were still plenty busy and growing the company on our own terms and at our own pace. Lots of the bigger accounts we solicited would ask for a **written proposal**, which was basically everything we promised verbally to be put on paper with a signature. Types of equipment, pricing, references, service frequency, etc. Nothing binding. We had an agreement with our accounts that if we didn't do the job we proposed, or for whatever reason the company wanted to change vendors we'd pull out in two weeks.

Conversely, if we didn't like the account we would be able to do the same, something we never had to do. **Two weeks time for removing equipment is the norm.**

One year the bids came in and we decided to take a hard look at one. It was a new hi-way rest area being proposed twenty minutes south of us that lots of vehicles would have to pass through. We knew that the rest area north of that was doing tremendous volume so we put in a bid and were awarded the contract.

But instead of the area for the machines being right off the hi-way, the state decided to locate them in an obscure spot that got about 3% of the vehicles to stop in there. A total blunder by some not so smart government officials. We hung in there for a while wishing for the best but eventually pulled out our machines. We were told we wouldn't be able to bid another contract for two years for doing this which was fine by us. Four new machines placed in money making accounts made way more sense. It wasn't too long after that the facility was converted to register motor vehicles, which validated our decision.

> **Vending Company Inc**
>
> 46 Center Road
> Any City, NH 03543
> TEL: 555-654-2341
> vendingcompanyinc@comcast.net
>
> PURCHASE Direct
> 100 Technology Drive
> Any Town, NH 03772
>
> August 23, 2015
>
> Attention: Cheryl Jones
>
> Vending Company Inc has been providing 24 hour service to satisfied customers in southern NH since 1989. We currently run 3+ routes from our warehouse in Any City, NH. Vending Company Inc uses only state of the art vending machines with dollar bill acceptors and card readers. We sell only name brand products with competitive pricing.
>
> We would like to propose the installation of the following equipment at your location at no cost or obligation to PURCHASE Direct: (1) snack machine, (1) cold beverage bottle machine and (1) fresh food machine. All will have card readers.
>
> These machines will be serviced on a regular basis to your satisfaction.
>
> Pricing Examples:
> Beverage pricing to stay the same.
> Small snack bags .75, Large snack bags $1.00, Candy bars and Pastry $1.25, Gum & Mint .75.
>
> Thank you for considering Vending Company Inc to satisfy your vending needs!!
>
> Owners, Vending Company Inc

A P.V.I. proposal. Towards the end, Lynne did these with her eyes closed.

A BIG ACQUISITION AND WAREHOUSE

By the end of the nineties we had 160 plus accounts and gross sales of over 1 million dollars. Mostly all our accounts were good producers but we did have some small locations doing $40 or less a week, with little chance of growth. In the early days we would grab anything and everything to increase cash flow but now as veterans in the industry, we knew what we wanted and didn't want. We made a decision to sell these smaller accounts. There were a couple of one man vending operations that had a niche in this market and did quite well.

These locations were either snack, soda, or both, and no commissions. Speaking of commissions, I'd like to know what idiot came up with this idea. For the record, this crazy policy was being practiced before we started filling machines and still goes on today, though not as prevalent. I can understand a little kick back for the use of electricity in an account, but giving away a good percentage of your income is insane! I do not know of any other service oriented businesses that do this. In my opinion, probably vending's only real negative.

Most of these accounts were every other week, every third week and some monthly. The larger companies won't take these accounts and your customers will really appreciate the service. Fewer repair calls, and snack/soda machines are generally quick and easy fixes. Both of these guys worked 40 or so hours a week and brought home nice paychecks with very little stress. We sold these accounts for .65-1.00 on the gross dollar minus the cost of the product in the machines, money in coin mechs and a final cash out. Terms were 30% down with 30 months to pay at 0% interest.

Any other leads on similar accounts were passed on to these guys as well. I would say over the years we transitioned $80-$90k in gross sales to them and they're both still at it doing very well. The timing of the sale of those accounts couldn't have been better, because shortly after our friend Gerry called to say he was retiring. He asked if we were interested in buying him out and we were. We agreed on a price for the business that included real estate. Gerry and his brother Bill had a 4400 sq.ft. building on 1 and 1/3 acres in the vicinity of one of the larger airports in New England, a great property.

Great property on the airport.

And so you can see, plenty of space.

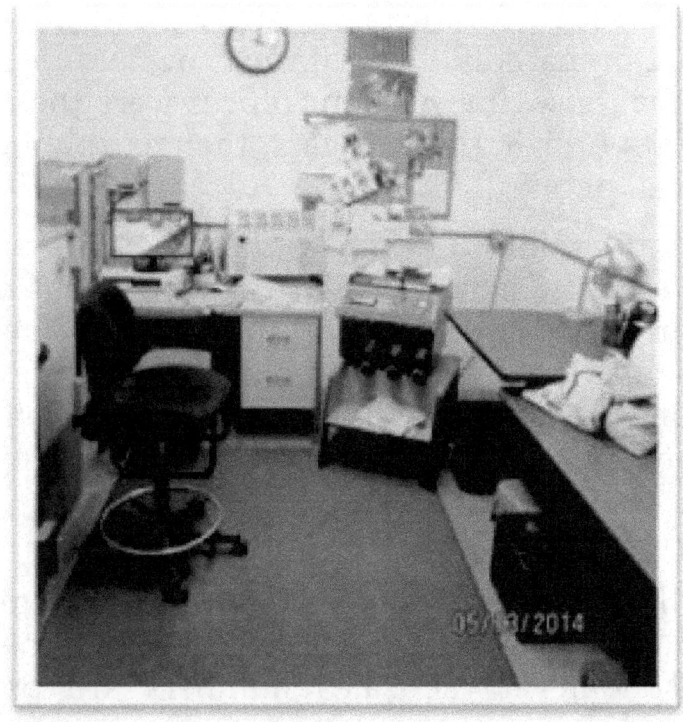

Designated money counting room.

Three vending routes with trucks and many extras like safes, hand trucks, pallet jacks, parts, tools and machines. The deal took forever to complete but after some beggin' and borrowin' from a local lender we were now at 6 routes doing gross sales of 2.1million a year with a prime piece of real estate. This was 2004 and 14 years after we had placed our first machine. No need to worry about local vendors calling because most were gone. For P.V.I. it was business as usual, with a few more headaches.

More employees, vehicles, machines and accounts but this suited us just fine. We picked up a couple more investment properties and were cruising along until a recession hit around 2007. This lasted until mid 2009 and forced us to take two trucks off the road but we made it through, because as I said, we always ran lean and were prepared for anything. As owners we always put in the most time and our offices were the cabs of our trucks utilizing first pagers, then car phones and finally cell phones.

It was a big relief to have two hard working women, our wives Lynne and Karla, taking care of business at the warehouse. I've known many small business owners that thought owning a business was a privilege and didn't have to work, but needless to say, when the economy tanks, they don't survive. If you keep your nose to the grindstone the vending business can be recession proof.

Try to have diversity in the types of accounts you service and if you're running multiple routes, be quick to consolidate if the sales numbers are trending downward. In many instances your numbers may go up because employees will forego leaving the workplace for lunch and use the vending machines for a quick fix before leaving for dinner at home. You may want to stretch out service frequencies in some locations as well but discuss this with your contact first.

FINAL ACQUISITION

Once the economy was back on track we negotiated our final acquisition with another vendor looking to retire, Andy of A&R Vending. We agreed on a fair price for his route which was around 25 stops and kept him on as a part-time employee. A veteran in the industry, he was a great addition, never missed a day and could do repair calls as well. The irony of this deal was A&R Vending was also my old neighbor Rick, the guy that didn't follow up on the lead I gave him years ago that would become our first vending account, H&M Metals. A&R had a falling out and Andy had been running the business by himself. Talk about coming full circle. During this time period we upgraded our moving truck to a 2002 GMC rack body with a plow. The lot at our warehouse was costing us $125 per storm and it didn't take long to realize the savings doing our own snow removal there and at our other properties.

Another plus for this acquisition was A&R used **quality equipment like Automated Products (AP), Crane Merchandising (National), Automated Merchandising Systems (AMS), U Select It (USI), Dixie Narco and Royal Vendor soda machines.** These are the manufacturers that I suggest you use. They have distributors across the country and are all good. After a while you may get a preference for one or the other but we've done well with all of them. **Vendor's Exchange (Cleveland, Ohio)** also sells new, used and completely refurbished machines of all types with favorable terms.

SEEN SOME CHANGES

When we started this business, it was pretty simple as far as the products to put into the machines and payment systems available to purchase those products. It was basically 12oz. aluminum cans, candy bars, small bags of chips, pastry, gum and mints. And as stated before, the advent of dollar bill acceptors. All the players in this industry never stop working on bigger, better and more. The bottling companies first attempt at 16oz. bottles was a disaster, resulting in constant jams due to its shape.

It wasn't long before they got it right with 20oz. and a better contoured bottle for dispensing. This led to far fewer service issues. The snack makers introduced **LSS bags (large single serve) and king size candy bars.** This was great for vendors because bigger items bring in bigger profits. Other distributors were packaging items like aspirin, dental and shaving products and just a wide array of items we had never seen early on in our career.

You can get top dollar for these products and they have long expiration dates. Schools placed restrictions on what we could sell and the suppliers did a great job introducing low fat, low sugar heart healthy items that actually taste pretty good. But the chubby kids are still chubby because they'll buy three bags instead of one and still don't walk to school, while the fit kids buy one bag and exercise daily. Hopefully one day the Feds will figure this common sense issue out.

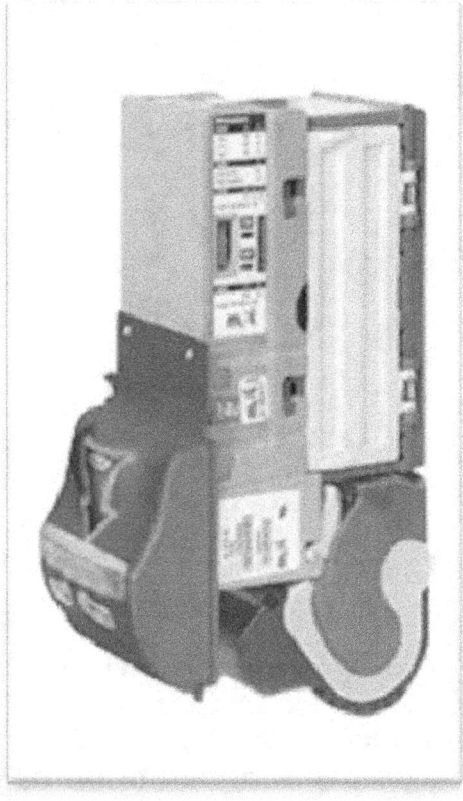

M.E.I. bill recycler. Still relatively new but again, made by a great company.

Equipment manufacturers went from one dollar bill acceptors to also accepting 5's, 10's, 20's and even a validator called **a bill recycler that will dispense bills instead of lots of coin when one of the forementioned currencies is used**. Coin mechs went from three tubes to four and then five tubes which did a good job eliminating use correct change issues.

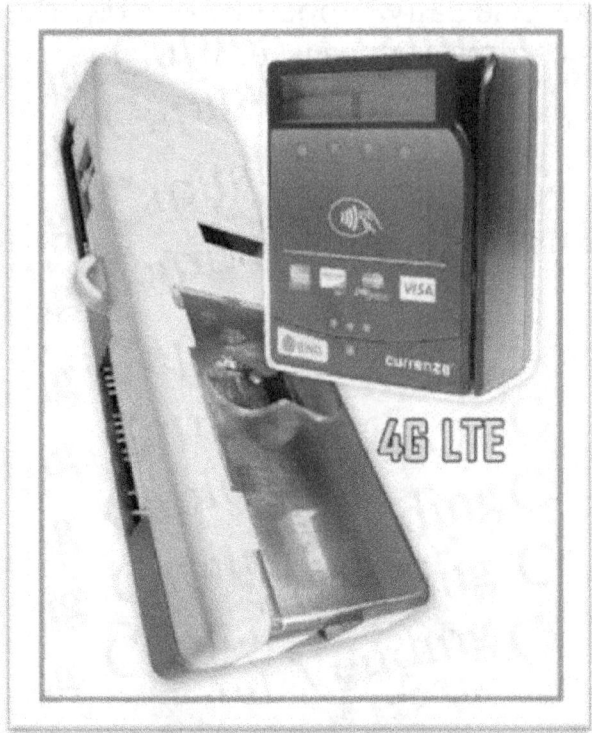

Crane card reader kit. Good stuff.

A major step, and as big as the dollar bill acceptor was in the nineties, was the introduction of **credit card readers**. These came out towards the end of our careers but every new account we installed had one and if the account didn't warrant one, we wouldn't take the location. We also spent considerable time and effort installing them on all our machines in the field and found a 30-40% increase in sales. Cash is still king, but today most people don't carry it so card readers are a must for any decent account. Cuts back on service calls too with less coin and bill jams.

There are a couple different card reader companies out there but we chose **Crane National,** a good company that sells quality machines as well. They have a nice lease to own program with warrantees that allow for a quick exchange if a unit fails. **Pre kitting** was another change a lot of the bigger companies were starting to adopt. You'll need updated or new software in your machines as well as cell service.

This program allows the home office to generate a sales report from a particular machine determining what items and the amount needed for the next delivery day. Route drivers have an app on their cell phone and a cable that is inserted into a portal on the control board of the machine that transmits the data to the office. Bins and soda cases are filled accordingly at the warehouse after the reports are read and put on the trucks for the next delivery. This improves accountability, cuts back on damaged products, identifies best sellers and allows drivers to service many more machines on their route. This procedure is something you'd probably want at least three routes before trying in my opinion.

THINKING OF SELLING? NAH

From the time we had 3 routes established until the year we sold (2018), we would get calls to sell the business. Most would be from big players in the Northeast like Next Gen (now gone), Service America (also gone) and Canteen franchises that was if anything, a nice learning experience. These guys would offer anywhere from .25-.40 on the gross dollar of yearly sales.

Not enough money for us and really not the right time. P.V.I. was operating 4 routes and everything was moving along just fine. All of our customers were loyal because we took care of business. Many times our contacts would give us a competitor's business card that was left with them. It was always thanks but we're all set with P.V.I. We were hands on running routes, doing service calls, or setting up new locations and we did this for 30 years.

We knew our customers and they knew us. If you run your business this way you will always have an edge over competition. Companies want to run their own business, the last thing they want to do is change the vendors every other year. In our third decade we had to make a hard decision, whether or not to get into the **micro-mart** side of the business.

Micro-marts are basically small convenience stores set up in the break room, no machines except for bean to cup coffee. Glass front coolers, freezers, open racks for dry goods like chips and candy and a **kiosk** for scanning purchases. Customers have the ability to examine whatever they're going to buy and the vendor can sell any size package they want, especially larger items that wouldn't fit into a vending machine. Large bags of beef jerky, chips, fresh fruit, large servings of ice cream, etc. Just about anything you'd find in a C-store.

Micro-mart or a small convenience store.

Unlike standard vending machines, pricing doesn't have to be in 5 cent increments which means you can sell a cup of coffee for $1.89 or a large sub for $5.99. The target application for this is white collar workers and lots of them. Pros are higher margins, fewer service calls and much more variety. Cons are these are not cheap to set up, you should have at least 3 to make it feasible and some people forget to pay (called **shrinkage)**.

You can count on a loss of 1-2.5% on an average per location, even with cameras. We were lucky because when these first came out our biggest accounts weren't interested and we really didn't want to get involved in another concept at that stage of our career. We had been at this for a while and knew it wouldn't be long before we seriously considered selling the business. Had **micro-marts** arrived 3-4 years earlier we more than likely would have gotten involved. As it turned out, we did lose two good accounts because of our game plan but were able to replace most of that revenue with traditional vending accounts.

There's no doubt micro-marts are here to stay but they will never replace vending machine service. With the downsizing of many workplaces the numbers just don't work for micro-marts but will always for one or two vending machines. Just starting out I'd stick with machines and markets will come later but if you're considering buying a company that already has some don't let it be a deal breaker. Service is still the name of the game and marts are actually easier to maintain than a **bank (full line)** of vending machines.

If you happen to get to the point where you have a market opportunity these are some to consider: **3 square, Avanti or CK Markets**. Please keep in mind though that this is a different animal. Yes, you're selling refreshments in the workplace but doing more merchandising with more products. All markets are pre kitted and all products must have **bar codes** for the purpose of scanning at the kiosk. I would also suggest that your markets be serviced by one designated route driver. These are tremendous money makers once you're comfortable in the industry so again, don't shy away. For us, the timing wasn't right but if you do get into the vending business, just go off your gut feeling. The players in this industry, manufacturers, suppliers, and distributors, are all great to work with and will advise you along the way.

SELLING? YEAH, AND A FINAL MOVE

As we were nearing the end of our third decade running P.V.I., we were steady at three heavy routes and beginning to seriously think about selling. I was 62 and Tom was 57 and we weren't getting any younger having a combined 75 years in the soda/snack industry. Very rewarding but also a toll on the body. In 30 years I had one sick day and Tom had zero, something I'm reminded about now and again.

Our warehouse at the airport wasn't being used to it's capacity and we had found a smaller one 5 miles away with a house on the lot as well. The rent income from the house would pay the mortgage so we'd be rent free with warehouse space. We got a good offer for the airport property and made the move. With half the space in our new location, we installed a shelter garage for cold storage of machines and equipment. A little tight but we made it work and being rent free was nice. The contact at one of our accounts that we knew for years asked me one day how much longer was I planning on filling vending machines. Joking, I asked why and if he wanted to buy the company.

I was surprised when he said yes. I told him we'd think about it and two months later we started talking. After several meetings bouncing around some numbers we agreed on the terms and decided to sell. The buyer's name was Chris. The sale consisted of 3 route trucks (Dodge Hi-Tops), 1 GMC rack body with plow, a fork truck, 6 **hand trucks (dollys)**, 2 pallet jacks, cash counters, a safe, **cardboard compactor**, walk-in freezer, office furniture and a 30 year collection of parts. A separate transaction was for inventory in the warehouse, product in the machines and coin mech money.

Cardboard compactor and a great investment where you'll never lose.

Dodge HiTop. These were the last route trucks we used.

I was to stay on board for one year with salary but ended up staying for two. In the middle of changing ownership, we received the bid for vending service in the state's university system. Chris decided to submit a bid and P.V.I. was awarded the contract which immediately doubled yearly gross sales. The length of the contract is for 5 years with an option for 5 more. Lots of work but lots of money. Not a bad first account for someone just getting into the business. Tom and I have since retired from vending operations after a combined 75 years of service. Tom is a salesman in another industry and I do some consulting work in yeah you guessed it, vending. A salesman for one of the manufacturers we bought lots of equipment from named Dennis, told me in 1990 that this was a great business and that I would never leave it. And you know, he might just be right.

CONCLUSION

Obviously, Tom and I had a unique path that led us into the vending industry but like any other service oriented business, we worked it hard to be successful. Vending machines aren't leaving the planet soon. Yeah, some are being replaced with micro-marts but that's such a small segment of the workplace.

Covid has set most industries back a bit but this is temporary. Imagine having human beings selling refreshments in breakrooms across the country? Most all of them would be unemployed. The vendors I know suffered a big blow too but will soon bounce back.

Consolidating routes, changing and or moving machines and following sanitary protocol might be the norm moving forward but this is a very resilient business, mainly because most all your employees are machines. You can put them to work for you pretty much wherever you want, they'll work all day and are always polite to the customers. So if you've been thinking about getting into the vending business part or full-time, I encourage you to go for it. Just remember to use the right equipment, keep 'em clean, filled and working…and if they're not working, fix them fast.

Be neat in appearance,

get the job done,

know your contact and remember

the customer is always right.

Good luck.

GLOSSARY

Automatic Merchandising Systems (AMS): Made in USA vending machines that are worth a look

Automatic Products (AP): Made in USA vending machines that are worth a look

Bar Codes: Funky little lines and numbers that are on pretty much any item that is scanned for purchase (think self check out)

Betson: Headquartered in New Jersey, distributors of vending and amusement machines, as well as parts

Bill Jam: When paper money doesn't get accepted all the way into a bill stacker and must be physically removed

Bill Recycler: Accepts 1's, 5's, 10's, and 20 dollar bills for purchase and can be programmed to return paper money as well as coin

Bill Stacker: A compartment of the bill acceptor or validator that holds the bills

Card Reader: A component that allows credit cards to be used to purchase from a vending machine

Cash Out: Emptying the money from a machine after it's serviced

Coin Counter: A valuable piece of equipment that will count coin for you when you get sick and tired of doing it by hand

Coin Jam: Pretty much the same as a bill jam except with coin and can occur anywhere from the mouth of the coin chute down into the coin mechanism

Coin Mechanism or Mech: Accepts coins for purchase and the first place you're going to look for a lot of your service calls

Cold Call: When you're on the hunt for new business and you just knock on a door, no appointment. Try it, it works. But please wear a mask

Cold Food Vendor: A heavy refrigerated vending machine that is used for fresh and or frozen food. We feel the Shoppertron by Crane Merchandising is the best

Commission: Similar to a bid, this is money given back to a location based on sales from the machine(s). The amount is usually anywhere between 5 and 15%. Note, not every location will ask for one so unless it's an account you must have, obviously don't bring it up

Cardboard Compactor: We leased to own one of these and it was one of our best moves. Takes all your cardboard and bales it, right around one ton. Shop for another user that will take it away and pay you when times are good. Not so good times, they'll still take it and you won't get as much but it beats paying for a dumpster. Another no brainer

Contact: Your liaison in an account. The person in charge of the vending. Get their ass fat with free chips and sodas and then kiss it. If they don't like you, you won't last long. And if they leave, get to know the new one, fast

Correct Change: When you see this it usually means one of the coin tubes in the coin mech is low or empty. Could also mean a coin jam anywhere in the mech and I've even seen a bill jam be the cause, but not often

Crane National: Made in USA vending machines that are worth a look. Check out their card readers too

C-Store: Convenience Store as in 7/11 or any other brick and motars with a gas pump, refreshments and lottery tickets

Dixie Narco: Made in the USA soda machines that are worth a look

Dollar Bill Acceptor (AKA Validator): A component on the front of a machine that accepts bills for purchase and another hot spot for service calls

Electric Stair Climber: Not what the name implies, you don't have to plug into an outlet to use but when not in use, should be plugged in to hold a charge. Expensive to own and not the easiest piece of equipment to operate, we never used one and left that application up to the pros. Wise move.

Full Line (AKA Bank) of Equipment: Usually found in larger locations consisting of several machines in a line. An example would be a snack, coffee, 2 sodas, food, bill changer and micro wave stand

Full Service: Just what it implies, the vendor fills the machines and cashes out. Some locations may have their own machines, buy product from you, fill them and keep the money themselves. This is not full service

Hand Truck (AKA Dolly): Arguably one of the greatest inventions of mankind, if you've worked yourself or watched anyone work. It's that piece of equipment made of metal with two small tires, a blade and a handle that allows cases of product to be moved around and pulled upstairs or lowered downstairs. When you get to your first stop and see that you forgot your hand truck, go back and get it or it will be a long day

Kiosk: Basically the end of the line when shopping and it's time to pay. Most likely will have some type of screen you'll scan the bar code over. Did you know that a phone booth is considered a kiosk?

LSS: Stands for Large Single Serve and is a bag of chips bigger than the typical vend size that will make you more money. Wish those were around when they didn't care what we put in the schools

Micro Mart: Picture a very small convenience store in the employee break room. No machines except for coffee. The rest of the equipment will be coolers, freezers, racks for chips and a kiosk for purchases. No bill acceptors or coin mechs so you'll have less service calls and no space limitations for any packages you want to sell. The latest and the greatest but not cheap and obviously built for high volume accounts. Don't be surprised when an item or two doesn't get scanned

OCS (Office Coffee Service): Again, just what it implies, a coffee service for the office employees. Usually free. Lots of accounts use different applications for coffee service throughout their building. Most offices will use a plumbed in **Bunn** or **Newco** (very good companies) that will fill pots or carafes automatically, some will use **K-Cups, pods, or a bean to cup machine**. Be careful here. Ever changing machines, coffee brands and pricing can make for a tough market

Pre Kitting: Fairly new to the industry but basically a report is generated from machine to route driver to office computer determining product levels or pars for that particular machine. The product is then picked at the warehouse and put in bins and or carts for the following service visit. The result, route drivers can fill more machines and know what's selling and what's not, less inventory in the warehouse, less damaged product, and greater accountability

Proposal: A short summary written for a potential new account stating pricing, types of equipment to be used, commission info if need be and anything else the contact would like on paper. And signed of course

Revision Door: Also fairly new and genius idea. Brand new doors with all updated control boards, lights, motors, etc. that can be put on most any dated machine in the field at a much lower cost than new

Royal Vendors: Made in the USA soda machines that are worth a look

Satellites: A small area in a large location that may need one or two machines because of proximity to the main breakroom, or a big hunk of metal up in the sky that's probably reading this too

Service Mode: A function, usually reached by pressing a button on the main control board of a machine that will allow you to do all kinds of stuff to that machine. Price it, free vend it, time it out, put a message on it and much more. But please, read the instruction manual first because if you hit the wrong buttons, that machine can do some crazy things

Shop: No, not that kind of shopping, but old school for warehouse. And remember, what goes on at the shop... you know

Shrinkage: Really, another word for not paying at a micro mart. Yeah it does happen, to the tune of an average of 1.8% per account. Even with cameras. Nice country America

Snack Stix: This one's special for me because we almost got sucked in... and you wouldn't be getting this vital information today. 1-800 Florida numbers for a package of vending machines that will even be placed in locations. With lying referrals as well. Still going on today so heads up

U Select- it: Made in the USA vending machines that are worth a look. The anti Snack Stix

Vendor's Exchange: Based in Cleve., Ohio a complete store for all your vending needs. Machines new, used or refurbished and a myriad of parts, accessories and tools. A tremendous company to do business with

ABOUT THE AUTHOR

Greg received his high school diploma in 1974 and spent the next 6 years languishing in college, garnishing enough credits to be just short of an associates degree in three or four different majors. At the end of the sixth year, with a GPA hovering around 1.7, he decided it might be a better idea to enter the workplace and start making money instead of wasting his parents while chasing a college degree. Greg started working for UPS in the late seventies and later had a couple of stints in public works. In the summer of 1983 he landed a job with Coca-Cola where, unbeknownst to him, would acquire the experience needed to start and operate a successful vending business.

The author with Trudy.